DAN DA DAN

STORY AND ART BY
YUKINOBU TATSU

7

CHARACTERS

MOMO AYASE

A high school girl from a family of spirit mediums. Her powers awakened after she was abducted by aliens. Following the battle with Turbo Granny, she helps to search for Okarun's testicles.

OKARUN (KEN TAKAKURA)

A geek for paranormal phenomena who lost his testicles in the fight against Turbo Granny and must now spend his time looking for them. He has developed feelings for Momo.

TURBO GRANNY

Appearing at unexpected times and places, she's a present-day yokai who ran riot throughout the country. Her power remains within Okarun, while her consciousness is stuck in a beckoning-cat figure that she uses to get around.

JIJI (JIN ENJOJI)

Momo's friend since childhood. He recruits Momo and Okarun to investigate and exorcise the spirits in his family's new house. But before they can, his body is possessed by the Evil Eye, a boy who'd been sacrificed under the house and became a yokai.

AIRA SHIRATORI

A popular, attractive girl at Momo's school whose powers awaken when she unknowingly picks up one of Okarun's family jewels. She ends up taking on the aura of the Acrobatic Silky.

TARO

An anatomical-model yokai who is dating anatomical model Hana. At present he has Jiji, currently possessed by the Evil Eye, trapped inside his own body.

MANJIRO

A priest at the Tsuchinoko Shrine near Jiji's home. He is also Seiko's disciple.

SEIKO

Momo's grandmother. She's active as the spirit medium Santa Dodoria. She's powerful enough to enclose their home in a mystical barrier, and she supports Momo and the others from the shadows.

STORY

Momo, a firm believer in spirits, comes to the rescue of a paranormal fanatic named Ken Takakura, aka Okarun, when he's getting bullied. After arguing about the validity of each other's interests, they decide to prove their respective beliefs, so Momo is sent to an abandoned hospital known for UFO sightings and Okarun heads to a supposedly haunted tunnel. Once there, Okarun gets cursed by a yokai called Turbo Granny! At the hospital, Momo ends up abducted by aliens called Serpoians, who are seeking a human female for reproduction. They take her aboard their ship, and Momo finds herself in big trouble. Suddenly, Okarun appears, and thanks to Turbo Granny's curse, he's able to transform. At the same time, Momo awakens to her paranormal abilities, and the two are able to escape the UFO. But Okarun's curse affects those around them, so they decide to have a showdown with Turbo Granny. Seiko sets up a barrier around Kamikoshi City, and Momo and Okarun subsequently beat Turbo Granny through a game of tag. Later, Jiji, Momo's old childhood friend and first crush, shows up troubled with supernatural problems of his own occurring in his family's new home, so Okarun and Momo head there to investigate. However, there are legends of a giant serpent in the area. In fact, the Kito clan has been secretly sacrificing humans to it under Jiji's new home, and they toss the young trio into an underground alternate reality as the latest offering. There the three find the serpent as well as a sacrificed child, now an Evil Eye yokai who goes on to possess Jiji. Suddenly, Seiko appears, sealing Jiji's possessed body inside the anatomical-model yokai Taro with a plan to exorcise it. Will Jiji get his body back, or is it too late to separate them?!

50. Let's All Carry Around Hot Water

EACH OF YOU...

...KEEP A HOT-WATER THERMOS ON YOU...

...SO YOU'RE PREPARED TO SPLASH HIM AT ANY TIME.

WE HAVE NO CHOICE BUT TO USE THESE.

WHEN YOU WASH YOUR HANDS, DRINK WATER, GO OUT IN THE RAIN...

YOU TAKE PLENTY OF CARE TOO, JIJI.

THE SLIGHTEST BIT OF COLD WATER WILL CAUSE YOU TO TRANSFORM.

YOU GOT THAT RIGHT.

I DON'T EVER WANT TO DEAL WITH IT AGAIN.

WE'VE GOTTA BE VIGILANT...

...UNTIL WE CAN COMPLETE THE EXORCISM!

WHERE WILL YOU LIVE, SHRIMP ALIEN?

I'LL BE LIVING AND WORKING AT A NEARBY DAIRY FARM.

THANKS TO MISS SEIKO.

HOW DOES THAT UFO ACTUALLY FLY?!

IS IT AN ANTI-GRAVITY PROPUL-SION SYSTEM?!

IT'S 🗣️!

BY THE WAY, SHRIMP, SIR...

WHAT'S YOUR NAME?

ER...

ON EARTH IT WOULD BE PRO-NOUNCED...

IF ANYTHING COMES UP, FEEL FREE TO CALL ON ME AGAIN.

THANKS FOR COMING TO OUR RESCUE!

HOOH! HOOH!

UM, MR. SHRIMP?!

...PEENY-WEENY.

LOVE

SURE!

PLEASE LET ME RIDE IN YOUR UFO SOME TIME, MR. SHRIMP!

WELL, SEE YOU LATER, MR. SHRIMP!

IS EVERY-BODY IN?

SEE YA LATER, L'IL CHIQUI!

GET LOST, SHRIMP!

HATE

ODEN LOVE

RIGHT HERE!

OKARUN!

GOT MINE!

DO YOU ALL HAVE YOUR THER-MOSES?!

AND HOT WATER?!

COOL.

NICE AND FULL!

IT'S OKAY!

OH. OKAY...

YOU'RE WORRYING TOO MUCH!

OH. SORRY...

JUST LEAVE YOUR HAND THERE.

OKAY.

STEP

STEP

TAP

TAP

WHAT?

I'M NOT DOING ANYTHING.

UM... MISS AYASE...

WHAT ARE YOU DOING?

AW, SHUCKS, WHAT'RE YOU TALKING ABOUT?

I MEAN YOUR HAND...

WHATEVER THE GAME IS, I DON'T KNOW THE RULES...

BUT WHY IS HE STANDING LIKE A BOARD?!

TARO, YOU NEED TO GET THAT BODY MOVING PROPERLY!

THANK GOODNESS!

THEY SEEM WELL!

YUP!

THAT'S EASY FOR YOU TO SAY, BUT MOVING THE BODY BY ITSELF AIN'T EASY!

HOW OFF-PUTTING.

GAH! YOU'RE MAKING A MESS OF IT!

GIVE ME BACK MY BODY!

SYNCH UP THE MOVEMENTS WITH JIJI!

HOWEVER, THE LEVEL FOUR ALERT WILL CONTINUE TO REMAIN IN EFFECT.

AT PRESENT, THE WILDFIRES ARE ALSO UNDER CONTROL...

THERE WERE NO CASUALTIES FROM THE ERUPTION.

...HAVE BEEN ARRESTED ON SUSPICION OF MURDER AND ABDUCTION.

IN RELATED NEWS...

JUICHI KITO AND TEN OTHERS LIVING IN DAIJA, AKA SERPENT CITY...

POLICE ARE SEEKING HER WHERE-ABOUTS.

...IS CUR-RENTLY ON THE RUN.

NAKI KITO SUSPECTED RINGLEADER

FURTHER-MORE, THE SUSPECTED RINGLEADER, NAKI KITO, AGE UNKNOWN...

HEF!

HEF!

HEF!

MOMO
AYASE
!

YOU
WON'T
GET
AWAY
WITH
THIS!

SHIT!

AND AFTER
SPENDING
200 YEARS
GETTING IT
THAT BIG!

51. We Can All Stay There Together!

THEY'RE NEEDED IN ORDER TO KEEP THE EVIL EYE ENTERTAINED.

YOU KNOW THOSE HAYASHI PERFORMERS THEY HAVE AT, LIKE, FESTIVALS AND STUFF?

APPARENTLY THAT MAKES IT EASIER TO EXPEL IT FROM THE BODY.

WE'LL HAVE TO KEEP IT IN CHECK OURSELVES.

SO IF TARO'S BARRIER STOPS BEING EFFECTIVE, THEN WE'LL HAVE TO DEAL WITH THE EVIL EYE AGAIN?!

BUT IT SEEMS LIKE THERE AREN'T ANY AROUND TO PERFORM THE HAYASHI MUSIC FOR US.

BY THE WAY, THERE'S A FAVOR I WANTED TO ASK, OKARUN.

WHAT'S THAT? AN ALIEN?

HUH? WHAT ABOUT THE GIANT EARTH-WORM?

V!! News
Volcanic Eruption! Is That A UFO?

LOOK, SEE!

THEY'RE SAYING A UFO WAS NEAR IT!

...SHE WON'T GIVE ME ANY MONEY FOR A PHONE.

MY GRANDMA BUYS MY UNIFORMS AND STUFF, BUT...

DON'T GOT ANY DOUGH!

I COULDN'T GET A HOLD OF YOU!

ANYWAY, WOULD YOU BUY A NEW CELL ALREADY?!

PLEASE DON'T BADMOUTH MOMO AYASE.

I WAS THE ONE WHO SPREAD THOSE LIES.

!!!

AIRA, WHAT'S UP?

GOT A SEC TO CHAT?

CUT THE ACT.

COME WITH US.

W-WHAT IS IT...

...MISS AYASE?!

SHUT IT!

LET'S GO. QUIT GRIPING ALREADY!

LET GO OF ME!

WHAT'RE YOU GONNA DO?!

I MEAN, JUST THE THOUGHT OF IT...

THIS IS THE WORST!

...MAKES ME SICK.

WELL, I GUESS THERE'S NO OTHER WAY...

CAN'T BE HELPED.

THIS TOTALLY SUCKS!

WHY HAS IT COME TO THIS?!

AGH! NO, NO, NO!

...

I GUESS IT'S UNAVOIDABLE, HUH?

C'EST LA VIE, AS THEY SAY...

WE'LL DO IT!

IF YOU CAN'T, THAT'S FINE. I'LL—

AIRA, IF YOU'VE GOT PLANS WITH FRIENDS, YOU CAN COME OVER WHENEVER.

HOW ABOUT STARTING TONIGHT?

TO-NIGHT?!

COOL!

HUH?! WHAT DO I DO?!

HUH?

...YOU DON'T HAVE TO FORCE YOURSELF TO HANG OUT WITH ME.

AIRA, IF SOMETHING'S GOING ON BETWEEN YOU AND YOUR FRIENDS BECAUSE OF ME...

NO...

I DON'T NEED TO HEAR THAT FROM YOU.

NOTHING LIKE THAT.

...

IT'S MY FAULT...

YOU'VE GOT NOTHING TO DO WITH IT.

AH!

THE ARM'S COME OFF.

JIJI, FROM HERE ON OUT, YOU'LL HAVE NO SUPPORT.

YOU NEED TO BE EVEN MORE CAREFUL OF WATER THAN YOU HAVE BEEN.

ONLY WASH YOUR HANDS IN HOT WATER.

RIGHT!

YOU SAVED ME!

THANK YOU, TARO!

GEEZ, AM I BUSHED!

I'VE BROUGHT THE WHOLE GANG.

PARDON THE INTRUSION!

I'M HOME!

AH.

YOU'RE BACK. PERFECT.

PRICEY! COULD YOU LET ME USE SOME LATER?

SKK GOLD EXPERIENCE.

WHAT SKIN LOTION DO YOU USUALLY USE?

SURE THING. IN THAT CASE, LET'S ALL PLAY TOGETHER.

I'M REAL GOOD.

OKARUN, LET'S PLAY SMASH BROS. AFTER.

MASSIVE BATTLE!

I TOLD YOU, I DON'T KNOW WHERE IT IS!

MY FLUFFY CUSHION. MOMO.

AH. YES.

HEY, FOUR-EYES, PASS THE SOY SAUCE.

THIS IS THE HOME OF SEIKO AYASE, ISN'T IT?

OH, I SEE!

WELL, WE'RE HERE TO FULFILL YOUR REQUEST.

SO WHAT IF IT IS?

WE'RE THE HAYASHI PERFORMERS.

IS THIS A JOKE?

THEY'RE SO COOOL!

WICKED! THEY'RE NOT WHAT I EXPECTED...

I'M KINDA EXCITED!

BUT THEIR PERFORMANCE IS THE REAL DEAL.

THEY HAVE THE POWER TO MAKE THEIR SOUND REACH EVEN THE REALM OF THE DEAD.

SO THEY'RE SPIRIT MEDIUMS?

NO.

THEY'RE NOT EVEN SPIRIT SENSITIVE.

HUH?

PLUS, THE LESS SPIRIT SENSITIVE THEY ARE...

...THE LESS LIKELY THEY ARE TO BE WON OVER BY EVIL SPIRITS DURING THE EXORCISM.

53. We Became a Family

DON'T KILL THE EVIL EYE!

...WE'D PLAY TOGETHER!

I PROMISED HIM...

HE JUST WANTS SOMEONE TO PLAY WITH!

HE JUST...

...ALL HE'S DREAMED OF IS THAT ONE DAY SOMEONE WOULD PLAY WITH HIM...

HE'S PRAC-TICED DANCING...

HE'S BEEN LOCKED AWAY FOR AGES...

...BUT EVEN STILL...

...IT'S ONLY TO GET KILLED AGAIN?!

...AND NOW, JUST WHEN HE THINKS HE'S FINALLY FREE...

I'LL BE SUPER CAREFUL NOT TO TOUCH ANY COLD WATER!

I'LL DO MY ABSOLUTE BEST!

DON'T KILL HIM! DON'T KILL THE EVIL EYE!

SO, PLEASE...

I'M *BEGGING* YOU!

I'M *BEGGING* YOU!

HUH?!

I'VE CHANGED MY MIND.

THE EXORCISM'S OFF.

THERE'S JUST SOMETHING I LIKE...

IT'S THE WAY IT'S GOTTA BE.

YOU HEARD WHAT JIJI SAID.

GRANNY, ARE YOU SURE?!

...ABOUT WHEN JIJI SHOWS SPIRIT LIKE THAT.

WELL, YOU CAN COUNT ME OUT!

SO, WHAT? WE'VE GOTTA KEEP WATCH OVER HIM FOREVER NOW?

I DON'T WANT TO WASTE IT ON HIS SELFISH-NESS!

OUR TIME IS PRECIOUS.

IN THAT CASE...

...I'LL IMPROVE MYSELF ENOUGH THAT I CAN KEEP THE EVIL EYE IN CHECK.

IF I CAN GET TOUGH ENOUGH...

...THEN EVEN IF YOU DO MORPH...

...IT WON'T BE A PROBLEM.

YOU'D NEVER BE ABLE TO SLEEP PEACEFULLY AGAIN!

YOUR LIFE WOULD BE IN DANGER!

BUT THAT'S...

TAKAKURA, YOU'D GO TO ALL THAT EFFORT FOR HIM?!

THE CARD-BOARD'S COME OFF HERE.

HEY.

SURE.

THANKS, OKARUN.

THERE'S EVENING DEW.

STAY AWAY FROM IT, JIJI.

...I CAUSED A LOT OF TROUBLE FOR MISS AYASE AND THE OTHERS.

WHEN I WAS CURSED BY TURBO GRANNY...

BUT THEY WENT OUT OF THEIR WAY TO SEE I WAS TAKEN CARE OF.

THIS IS ALL MY FAULT. I'M SORRY.

PLEASE DON'T APOLO-GIZE.

WE'RE ALL IN THIS TOGETHER.

WHAT'S THE POINT OF PAYING ME BACK? MORON.

I PROMISED MYSELF I'D PAY BACK...

...THE LIVING EXPENSES AND CLOTHING COSTS, ET CETERA...

BUT THEN...

...SO I DELIVERED NEWSPAPERS AND BROUGHT HER SOME MONEY.

...YOU CAN PAY IT FORWARD BY HELPING SOMEONE ELSE WHO'S IN TROUBLE.

IF YOU'RE FEELING INDEBTED TO ME...

...FOR LOOKING AFTER YOU...

THAT'S WHAT BEING IN THIS TOGETHER REALLY MEANS.

BUT I'D LIKE TO BECOME EVEN A *LITTLE BIT* COOLER...

...SO I COULD BE LIKE HER.

I WISH I COULD SAY STUFF LIKE THAT...

DAMN, SHE'S SO AWESOME!

...BUT IN MY CASE, I'D JUST BE TRYING TO LOOK COOL.

CHIRP CHIRP CHIRP

YAWN!

MAYBE I'M COLD BECAUSE THE HOUSE IS.

YOU WERE SLEEPING WITH YOUR BELLY EXPOSED.

YOU SHOULD'VE COVERED ME, THEN!

UGH. MY TUMMY HURTS...

YES ...

TOTALLY PREPPED FOR TODAY'S LESSONS?

TAKAKURA, YOU DIDN'T FORGET ANYTHING, DID YOU?

SEE Y'ALL LATER!

SHUT YER FAT FACE...

...YOU DAMN LIAR!

WELL, YOUR TEETH GRINDING IS DEAFENING!

HEY, STOP THAT!

MOMO'S A REALLY RESTLESS SLEEPER!

TAKAKURA, LISTEN.

YOU TOLD ME I COULD!

AND SHE USES MY LOTIONS WITHOUT ASKING!

NO, IT WOULD NOT.

SO IF MOMO AND JIJI HAD TEA TOGETHER, WOULD *THAT* BE A DATE?

WOULDN'T YOU CALL THAT A DATE?!

WE'RE JUST GOING TO HAVE SOME TEA!

I DON'T GO ON DATES!

THEN WHAT'S THE DIFF, YOU PIECE O'...?!

MRF MRF MRF!

FINE! DON'T HAVE A SINGLE DROP THEN!

I WON'T!

YOU'LL GET THIRSTY.

I WON'T DRINK A SINGLE DROP OF TEA!

OKARUN! RIGHT HERE, RIGHT HERE!

I WILL NOT!

OKA-RUN!

WHUT THE...

MISS AYASE!

AAH!

THREE!

HOW MANY IN YOUR PARTY?

WELCOME BACK, MASTER!

...!

HEY, MAID LADY!

SERVE THIS CUS-TOMER!

EXCUSE ME. THAT MAID'S GOT A BAD ATTITUDE.

FINE. WELC'M.

THIS WAY.

MISS AYASE! BE MORE COURTEOUS!

YES, MA'AM...

AND SPEAK CLEARLY!

WELCOME TO OUR ESTABLISHMENT, YOU SACK OF SHIT.

SORRY! IT SLIPPED OUT!

YOU'RE SUPPOSED TO SAY, "WELCOME BACK"!

MISS AYASE! HOW COULD YOU?!

I THINK I'LL HAVE THE TEA.

HMM. LET'S SEE...

PURE APPLE JUICE.

MAY WE TAKE YOUR ORDER?

MISS AYASE'S MAKING ALL THIS EFFORT...

BUT I DO! I WANT SOME-THING!

HUH ?!

YOU DIDN'T NEED ANYTHING TO DRINK, RIGHT, OKARUN?

BUT YOU SAID BEFORE YOU DIDN'T NEED ANYTHING TO DRINK, TURD!

MOE!

MOE!

TRI-BEAM!

YOU BASTARDS! YOU'LL REGRET THIS, DAMN YOU!

I TOOK SOME ADORABLE PHOTOS OF YOU, MOMO!

NICE WORK YOU'RE DOING THERE!

WHO CARES?! YOU'RE A MAID!

YOU'RE SO CUTE!

YOU TOLD ME THE JOB WAS AT A RESTAURANT!

DID YOU JUST COME HERE TO MAKE FUN OF ME?!

55. Moe! Moe! Tri-beam!

WHAT'S UP?

OKARUN, LET'S GO.

GIVE IT YOUR ALL!

SEE YA. THANKS FOR YOUR SERVICE.

SHOO! SHOO!

LEAVE! GO!

ACTUALLY, I'M GOING TO STAY...

YOU'RE ON THE ROAD TO RENOVATING!

JIJI WILL BE WAITING FOR YOU.

OKARUN, YOU GOTTA GET OUTTA HERE ASAP.

HMMM?

HAVE FUN!

SORRY FOR BARGING INTO YOUR PLACE OF WORK.

YOU SHOULD BE!

DON'T EVER COME HERE AGAIN!

MISS AYASE, WHAT TIME ARE YOU HERE TILL?

GEEZ, IT'S COLD!

UH...

TEN.

HUH?!

ALL RIGHT.

THEN I'LL STAY HERE UNTIL YOU'RE DONE.

IT'S DANGEROUS FOR A GIRL TO GO HOME...

AND IT'S FREEZING. YOU'LL CATCH A COLD!

NO. I TOLD YOU TO LEAVE.

...ALONE AT NIGHT.

TAKE CARE.

OKAY, THEN...

I'LL BE FINE.

I'M TOUGH.

NUH-UH!

I... SEE...

REALLY?!

MOMO, YOU WERE REALLY GREAT TODAY!

THANK YOU FOR EVERYTHING!

SEE YOU AGAIN SOON, OKAY?!

I'M SORRY FOR ALL THE HEADACHES I CAUSED YOU!

YUP!

I'LL BE OFF, THEN!

TAKE CARE!

HUH. GUESS I'LL HEAD HOME, THEN.

ALL DONE WITH WORK?!

HUFF HUFF

HUH?! WAIT. YOU DIDN'T GO HOME?!

HUFF HUFF

MISS AYASE!

NOW LET'S GET HOME QUICKLY!

I CAN'T VERY WELL LEAVE A GIRL BY HERSELF AT THIS HOUR!

BRR, IT SURE IS COLD!

BECAUSE
IT'S COLD.

IT'LL BE OKAY.

BELIEVE IN YOUR-SELF.

OKAY. HERE WE GO.

THAT TOTALLY DRAINED ALL MY STRENGTH!

YIKES!

AMAZING! IS SUCH A THING EVEN POSSIBLE?!

THAT WAS CLOSE!

YOU'RE A REAL PRODIGY, YOU KNOW.

UN-REAL.

...BUT COLD ONES ARE STILL OUT.

YOU MAY BE ABLE TO HANDLE ROOM TEMPERATURE LIQUIDS...

DON'T DROP YOUR GUARD.

IT SEEMS YOU'LL BE ABLE TO RETURN TO NORMAL LIFE.

AT LEAST IT'S GOOD TO KNOW YOU'RE CAPABLE OF SUPPRESSING IT.

EVIL EYE! STOP!

FIGHT ME INSTEAD!

BZAK

GANZAN DAISHI

56. Feeling Kinda Gloomy

I'LL HAVE SOME OF THIS HOT WATER, IF I MAY.

THAT WAS CLOSE!

THANK GOD I DIDN'T SWALLOW IT!

IT WASN'T YOUR FAULT.

IT'S ALL RIGHT.

UH, IF I HELP, WILL YOU MAKE ME YOUR APPRENTICE?

THERE'S NO TIME TO BE PUTTING YOUR FEET UP.

EH?!

ANYWAY, COULD YOU TAKE THESE BAGS OVER THERE?

NO WAY.

WHY NOT ?!

WEEZ WEEZ

I WON'T... LOSE HEART!

NOT ME...

TOMOR-ROW, I'LL GET HIM TO TEACH ME TO PUNCH FOR SURE...

I'M BACK!

WE MANAGED SOMEHOW THIS TIME THANKS TO MISS MOMO'S QUICK WITS.

BUT THAT MOVE WON'T WORK AGAIN.

I MEAN, TRYING TO LIVE WITH AN EVIL SPIRIT IS WEIRD IN THE FIRST PLACE.

MANJIRO.

I'LL GO CONTACT THEM.

AGREED?

LET'S CALL FOR THE HAYASHI BAND AGAIN.

IF YOU WON'T PERFORM THE RITUAL PRAYER, MASTER...

...THEN I WILL.

IT'S A BITTER PILL.

IT'S ALSO AN ADULT'S RESPONSIBILITY...

...TO SHOW THEM REALITY.

AS AN ADULT, YOU WISH YOU COULD SHOULDER ALL YOUR KIDS' BURDENS YOURSELF...

...AND TELL THEM...

LOOK, I ADMIRE JIJI'S SPIRIT TOO.

BUT WHAT CAN'T BE DONE CAN'T BE DONE.

...TO DO WHATEVER THEY WANT.

HOW SAD...

EMPLOY A SNAPPING MOTION AND...

WHAT DANCE IS *THAT*?

LISTEN, YOU. WHY'RE YOU TRYING TO LEARN TO PUNCH?

PFFT!

CLUMSY SON OF A...

I'M NOT DANCING!

LEAVE ME ALONE!

BECAUSE I WANT TO TOUGHEN UP, OBVIOUSLY!

IT'S THE SAME.

OR DO YOU WANNA BECOME STRONG?

SO DO YOU WANNA LEARN HOW TO THROW A PUNCH?

I WANT TO LEARN...

...TO THROW A PUNCH SO I CAN BECOME STRONG.

NO. THEY'RE DIFFERENT THINGS.

THE EVIL EYE IS LEVELS ABOVE YOU IN POWER AND TECHNIQUE.

JUST BECAUSE YOU CAN THROW A PUNCH DOESN'T MEAN YOU'LL BE STRONG.

WHAT ?!

SO THEN WHAT AM I SUPPOSED TO DO?!

HE CAN EVEN KEEP UP WITH MY POWER.

HIS SPEED'S CONSIDERABLE TOO.

THAT IS YOUR *COMBAT RHYTHM.*

LOOK AT THAT DUMMY JUMP.

HEY!

WHAT'RE YOU TRYING TO DO HERE?!

AND THIS...

...IS THE EVIL EYE'S RHYTHM.

RHYTHM?

THIS IS
THE EVIL
EYE.

THIS IS
YOU.

TRUDUDAH
TRUDUDAH
TRUDUDAH

PLINK
PLINK
PLINK

GET
IT?

IN THE TIME
IT TOOK YOU
TO JUMP AND
LAND ONE
TIME...

PLINK

TAKING
YOUR
JUMPS
BEFORE
AS AN
EXAMPLE.

...WOULD
HAVE
COMPLETED
FOUR
DIFFERENT
ACTIONS.

...THE
EVIL
EYE...

TRUDUDUDUDAH

WHERE'S IT COMING FROM?!

AN OR-CHES-TRA?!

THAT NOISE!

IT'S SO LOUD, I CAN'T HEAR Y—

HERE?! WHAT'S HERE?!

THEY'RE HERE.

WHOOO'S MAKING THAT NOISE?!

I CAN HEEEAR SOME IMPURE SOUNNNDS.

SHE'S DODGING ALL OF THEM!

WOW! AIRA-CHAN IS AWESOME!

TUNK

THIS IS NO TIME FOR ADMIRATION!

YOU NEED TO DODGE LIKE THAT TOO!

AND I'M GOOD-FOR-NOTHING!

MISS SHIRATORI! SHE'S INCREDIBLE!

KOFF! KOFF!

HFF! HFF!

I'M NO BETTER!

BUT NOT AT ALL...

BWUH!

I THOUGHT I'D BECOME A BIT STRONGER...

I'VE FOUGHT A BUNCH OF TOUGH ENEMIES...

OH!

...AND I GOT INTO THE RHYTHM OF IT!

IT REALLY MOVED ME...

THERE *IS* SOMETHING! SOME MUSIC I HEARD RECENTLY!

SHIT! NO OPENINGS TO COUNTER-ATTACK!

EVEN WHEN I TRY EXTENDING MY HAIR...

...THE NOTES ARE HITTING IT SO IT DOESN'T REACH THEM!

Dandadan Vol. 7 End

HEY, MOMO! WHERE'S THE MILK?!

HOW SHOULD I KNOW?!

DON'T GIVE UP ON ME, OKAY?

...AFTER ALL.

YOU'RE STILL ALIVE...

End

KITO FAMILY

TYPE: HUMAN (?)
HABITAT: HOT SPRINGS DISTRICT
HEIGHT: 140-180 CM

A MULTIGENERATIONAL CLAN OF SELF-PROCLAIMED GUARDIANS OF A CERTAIN HOT SPRINGS AREA. OPERATING UNDER THE GUISE OF LANDLORDS, THEY BEHAVE OUTRAGEOUSLY AND WITHOUT CONSIDERATION. RESIDENTS AVOID THEM. THEY HAVE CONNECTIONS IN THE POLICE FORCE, SO ANY COMPLAINTS ABOUT THEIR CRIMINAL ENDEAVORS GET COVERED UP!

NAKI

JUMANUEL
JURIA
JUGEMU
JUHIKO
JUICHI

TYPE:
SUBTERRANEAN

HABITAT:
AGARTHA

HEIGHT:
180 CM (APPROX.)

SUBTERRANEAN

THE TRUE FORM
OF NAKI KITO, CURRENT HEAD OF THE KITO
FAMILY. ALL OTHER INFORMATION ABOUT HER
IS A MYSTERY.

YUKINOBU TATSU

I was overexuberant in my chewing of some Black Black gum, and somehow my tolerance for its spiciness has now increased.

Yukinobu Tatsu debuted in *Gekkan Shounen Magazine* with *Seigi no Rokugou* (Rokugou of Justice). He has also worked as an assistant for manga artist Tatsuki Fujimoto on the well-known series *Chainsaw Man* and *Fire Punch*.

DAN DA DAN

7

SHONEN JUMP Edition
Story & Art YUKINOBU TATSU

Translation/KUMAR SIVASUBRAMANIAN
English Adaptation/JENNIFER LEBLANC
Touch-Up Art & Lettering/KYLA AIKO
Design/JULIAN [JR] ROBINSON
Original English Logo Concept/SARA LINSLEY
Editor/JENNIFER LEBLANC

Printed in Canada

Published by VIZ Media, LLC
P.O. Box 77010
San Francisco, CA 94107

10 9 8 7 6 5 4 3 2 1
First printing, April 2024

viz.com

What happens when an unlucky girl meets an undead guy? *PURE CHAOS!*

UNDEAD UNLUCK

Story and Art by
Yoshifumi Tozuka

Tired of inadvertently killing people with her special ability Unluck, Fuuko Izumo sets out to end it all. But when she meets Andy, a man who longs for death but can't die, she finds a reason to live—and he finds someone capable of giving him the death he's been longing for.

JOJO'S

BIZARRE ADVENTURE

PART 5 *Golden Wind*

STORY & ART BY
HIROHIKO ARAKI

A MULTIGENERATIONAL TALE OF THE HEROIC JOESTAR FAMILY AND THEIR NEVER-ENDING BATTLE AGAINST EVIL

GOLDEN WIND is here! The highly-acclaimed fifth arc of Hirohiko Araki's *JoJo's Bizarre Adventure* shifts the action from Japan to Italy, as Koichi Hirose heads to Europe to find an aspiring gangster named Giorno Giovanna, the secret son of Dio Brando, scourge of the Joestar family. Organized crime meets family drama and unbelievable enemy Stands in *JoJo's Bizarre Adventure: Part 5—Golden Wind*!

See the origins of the mad genius
who created *CHAINSAW MAN*!

TATSUKI FUJIMOTO
BEFORE CHAINSAW MAN

Story and Art by Tatsuki Fujimoto

Short story manga collections featuring
Tatsuki Fujimoto's earliest work. It's rough,
it's raw, and it's pure Tatsuki Fujimoto!

CAN MUSCLES CRUSH MAGIC?!

MASHLE

MAGIC AND MUSCLES

STORY AND ART BY
HAJIME KOMOTO

In the magic realm, magic is everything—everyone can use it, and one's skill determines their social status. Deep in the forest, oblivious to the ways of the world, lives Mash. Thanks to his daily training, he's become a fitness god. When Mash is discovered, he has no choice but to enroll in magic school where he must beat the competition without revealing his secret—he can't use magic!

Kafka wants to clean up kaiju, but not literally! Will a sudden metamorphosis stand in the way of his dream?

KAIJU NO. 8

STORY AND ART BY **NAOYA MATSUMOTO**

Kafka Hibino, a kaiju-corpse cleanup man, has always dreamed of joining the Japan Defense Force, a military organization tasked with the neutralization of kaiju. But when he gets another shot at achieving his childhood dream, he undergoes an unexpected transformation. How can he fight kaiju now that he's become one himself?!

YOU ARE READING THE WRONG WAY

DAN DA DAN

Dandadan reads from right to left, starting in the upper-right corner. Japanese is read from right to left, meaning that action, sound effects, and word-balloon order are completely reversed from English order.